Concealed Nations

Joel Felix

Verge Books, Chicago

Concealed Nations

Copyright © 2020 by Joel Felix
All rights reserved
Published by Verge Books
www.vergebooks.com
ISBN 978-0-9889885-7-6
Cover image: exploded hollow point bullet. Expanding rounds like this are designed to stop inside the body and leave no exit wound.
Designed by Crisis
Printed in Michigan on acid-free, recycled paper

Fall 1 1

Tutor Song 5

Voice Box 6

"I WAS. I AM NOT. I DON'T CARE." 7

How Many Bubbles Are in a Bar of Soap? 9

Fullerton West from Cicero 11

Wolf Lake 12

Second Son 13

Mother Omen 14

Love Songs of Military Anthropology 19

Challenge Solve 20

Concealed Carry 21

Open Carry 29

Concealed Nations 31

Hecuba 32

The Measure 34

Fall 2 35

Science Is Suffering 39

Comment on the Emission Spectrum 40

Reproducibility Zoo 41

This Poem Takes Privileges 42

Infant with Love 43

Kill Chain 44

Broward 59

Walking Stick 61

Innertown 63

Burn It Up (after Sappho) 64

Stephen Crane 65

Whose Blues 66

Fall 3 67

Western Avenue 71

[. . .] AQUI VIVE 72

I Dreamed I Saw Ron Johnson Last Night 73

You Are Surrounded! 75

Landscape with Fill (after Joseph Ceravolo) 76

"eat shit beef" 77

Downriver 79

Poem for Tearing Away 80

Notes 83

Acknowledgments 87

Fall 1

I sat in a coffee shop, waiting for a friend I hadn't seen in years. I was anxious, and the legend on the nut bar wrapper was difficult to follow. The city was familiar yet felt from a great distance. I had lived here for years but just now had returned to give a talk. The Loop and landscape read as the architecture of a misplaced identity, a contagion of desire. I imagined arriving at the talk astride a dead dog to show this city that all its realities can be undone. The Loop was grinding at the noon hour's nerve with columns of passers-by, cars and cabs, shrieks of the elevated trains overhead. I re-read my talk with one eye, words moving by like people in their swollen pulps, bodies with deeper meaning than their charcoal silhouettes. I know you came here expecting poetry, I might say, but I cannot speak, as I am just a limestone lion, like you.

After the coffee, I hop in a cab at Wabash. *I'm heading to Manny's*, I tell the driver. *The Jewish place?* he asks. His driver's badge and ID are shrink-wrapped to the seat back. I'm guessing he's Pakistani? I say, *Yeah, you been there?*

Good place, he says, *good food.* I say, *Yeah, it's like home to me.* He looks back through the mirror: *You Jewish? No,* I say, as a simple fact. He pauses. *Good place,* he says again, *many drivers go there.* I sense I'm suddenly less relevant. He rejoins the conversation on his headset, and I sit back, pleased at the city in a hurry, the desires of the city rushing to love what I love. But the sense of rush halts; traffic clusters to a stop as we turn onto Wabash. The driver is angry, still speaking, to me? Or is his muttered, dull fury just for the windshield or the headset? *Where you from?* He stops muttering to reply, *Pakistan.* I ask, *How is it going in Chicago? It's hard,* he says, *you drive very hard, you work all the time.* He cuts traffic by heading east on Congress then dips into the alley that runs between Michigan and Wabash. I cluck my tongue over the risk we'll run into a blockade of delivery trucks and be forced to back out. Then I let it go. He's finding the fastest route for me. Maybe he's thinking that nothing can make today better than going to Manny's. Maybe we will shuffle together in the cafeteria line past the silent kreplach ladler, the stony beef carver, and the joyful pastrami forker. We'll sit near the table reserved for Axelrod and gaze at Obama portraits. My legs start tingling as the cab shoots out of blind alleys flanked by skyscrapers across the bustling sidewalk. *Watch the people,* I say, trying not to sound judgmental. The alleyway is clear and we're making good time as the cab barrels on and then bursts across the sidewalk of Harrison, nearly running down college kids emptying from a downtown campus. I gurgle with alarm as a young woman is nearly run over. She spins away and gives the cab driver the finger. *Did you see that? Did you see what she says to me?* Is the cab driver talking to me or someone on the headset? I say, *Yeah, that was too close . . .* then he guns the cab into the stopped traffic. The woman has gotten clear of the car, but now he's hopping in his seat, shouting out the window at her, *Who are you, who are you, what do you think? Who are you?* She turns back to him and yells, *Fuck you!* The cab driver floors the gas. There's a quick melt of tires. I'm thrown about in the back seat. We can't go forward into the wall of cars or back as pedestrians block the alley behind us. *Hey, Hey!* I yell unheard. He is just screaming now: *Who is she? Bitch! Who are you?* He gets out and runs at the sidewalk, his car door open in the congested street. Every horn blasts in sorrow at me in the back seat. The woman backs away, but he's gaining. She holds up her phone as if this might ward him off. He's right on her and I'm yelling *Hey! Hey! Forget about it, man! Forget about it!* People are taking cover. It seems he's heard me now and responds,

Who is she? I will beat her! I will beat her! My body has jumped out now after him with no idea what to do. Can I take him down? What then? She's trying to start recording a video and he slaps her arm away. He's got a hand on her coat. I'm right behind him about to jump and my ears suddenly open up—I can hear the cars honking again. His cab is left in the street. Maybe it's the only thing more important than his honor. *Hey man,* I yell, *someone just hit your cab, man, somebody just hit your car,* I say, my face sharing his pain, as if I too saw the inevitable destruction of the city we hoped for. He turns back, furious, and runs to confront the drivers honking at his cab. I say to the woman, *Just go! Go!* She runs. He's in the street screaming threats. Cars are going around. I duck into a diner and watch through the window. He's looking for her. She's gone. He's looking for me. I turn my back and look at the floor. Then he gets in the car and drives off, hard, like the only way to close this is crunching a body under that Chevy. What did I just do? What if she didn't want to run, but fight? Why did he tell me that he would punish that woman, as if I would be on his side? Is it worse or better that he has disappeared into the city? A few hours later I would give a talk, entitled "Fool for Love."

Tutor Song

*The poem
does not lie to us. We lie under its
law, alive in the glamour of this hour*

—heaven's flood
ladled this day
    the road held
like a child, you and
I;

you, John Wieners,
your arms around
my poem,
a solid cloud of smoke and water
blushing a ruby print
over this district
    defined as poor.

Voice Box

Arrest me, if I run away,
for my heart is not free

read the tattooed foreheads
of Cicero's slaves

as in Rome, as in the way
modern work happens.

When stopped, keep hands
in sight. Move slowly
and appear calm. If taken down

on the writhing street, scream

mine will be
its tongue.

"I WAS. I AM NOT. I DON'T CARE."
(A Gallic tombstone from the Roman Empire)

FOR ROBBIE

I hear in my voice a special development
in paganism, a motivation
for the space between
singer and ear where
all the monstrous find ready welcome
as ciphers of the State.

Squeeze hand
to extrude eardrums, turn out the pockets:

one man's hair comb,
one Timex digital watch,
broken, a prophylactic, unused,
twenty-three dollars and seven cents.

Sign here. Each comes, finally,
to his contents,
the constituent, unloved parts
upon release.

How Many Bubbles
Are in a Bar of Soap?

What you got today,
aluminum meal tray?

In walks an owl
to collect

meat and fur,
pieces of the road

that is me
for a moment, and then

will not be.

You go with who you are
as rain falls on hotdog buns

and other silent conditions
of the leasehold,

machine names assigned
to the stars and their babies,

cobbles in the mouth
of the sky cracked open.

Heaven needs
how many chains
to leash the Earth?

How many bubbles are in a bar of soap?

The form is forced answer
to all questions

intent on depeopling
human terrain

down to a Birmingham
bench set back from the street
next to no one.

Fullerton West from Cicero

Drop ceiling, vinyl wood panel,
ballast buzz,

carmaggedon's bright avenue
markets space for the curious

in the choreography
of Tae Kwon Do.

Wolf Lake

Ducks winter over
warm diesel-spotted
waters at the toll road
approach.

Bright winter berries
on the dash.

We have the car
and Jugo de Coco.

We lost much today
we don't want to know.

Second Son

Your hand is the weight of a paper cup
swollen in dream

lifting like the morning air
at the turn to noon—

Son, master in ventriloquy,
as all things speak.

We are *camped*
under a dying tree

    and when you see a cop,

        we run.

Mother Omen

My mother appears as an omen

when I rake my bag
for something to write on.

Her head turns to me
silent as Athena
at an altar imposed on this street.

In time, crackers, gum, and ink
merge to conjure her,
the child's tree, the first island
of her body

frustrated at the alchemies of purses
turned to tacky soil, our substance

matting the talismanic checkbook
charged to avoid danger

for just one smooth day.

Safety is fear; fear is safety, my mother, dear.
We populate the street with omens

that remake
parts of Wacker Drive I once walked

to work,
stung by salt-cracked January
washed in March
cigarette butt flotillas
in the flood drains.

Her omen returns when
all she hoped to make
is gone. In her, my body,

insatiate to conceive this pain
and urge it from life
into the be-dazed morning, as if nursing

a Tootsie Roll,

cracks the chitin
on this rainy transfer between trains

that captures me.

I blind-root
the bag, again, as if my fingers could be touched

by water snakes
alive in the lake bottom's cave,

as if a nāga deity,
might offer his body as a snake pen,

free the urgent gazelle inside
my chest,

a part that leapt
off early

to hunt the chrysanthemum's green eye
squared in concrete

one would remember as the garden
transmissions

behind the garage
the neighbors hate.

A fast twitch
pounds my blood in loose-

bound co-incidents,
the everyday cochlear nautiluses
created by choice or accident

as if the breath in your ear
was the living wash,

as if the thousand-fold mantle
would part like an afternoon

to make time bring you
her.

A dwarf oak
turns its eyes.

All omens have come
to remind me
of you, my mother,

who you were
and what you are
since you died, made

willing to believe in any and all

concealed nations,
cousins, enemies, and food,

hidden spirit medicines in
city crossings

alive in intervals
of the stotting gazelle

or inside me

and with your starving ghost
I feed and

stable.

Love Songs of Military Anthropology

Is that the smell of your skin, haunting
my shallow wrist,
and was that me,
standing by your bed
at dawn?

As Eros I took this man
and vowed to never
forget his desire
to make a dent in the suffering

with data on fresh produce availability
in the spread of terror groups.

It's a long wait for the people to get sick,
but only then will friendly community analysis
bring success in war.

Challenge Solve

If we do anything well, it's huddles

is one thing I take away from the meeting even if it may not be on the list

to do.

Pick up one thing and put down
another thing. You guys know this work. The model is to charge whatever we want

until the jobs go away.

Concealed Carry

Down the Oh
    hi
        O

taken away
on her bosom smooth

O take me down
the Ohio

my eyes go where you
want to go

all my sins
taken a-way.

Out in the river,
a ratty dock stares down

the low velocity effluvia
from a mouth that drains
fifteen states

concealed in the Devonian carnival of snail,
armored fish, and sea spiders going

the way of protected Kentucky nature
and real property,

speleogens from the cave boundary

on the gun-free zones
where creeping federal takeover

meets no resistance
from heritage farms or public building
trackways,

including,
or synonymous with,

but not limited to

anastomoses, scallops, rills, flutes, spongework, boxwork, pendants, and human remains,

the fur-bearing smorgasbord

our menu for living is turning to shit
and seed-plants have waited too long

without insect
or bird.

You might free a most interesting fossil—

whether the black of the negro resides in the reticular membrane between the skin and scarf-skin,

 *or in the scarf
-skin*

itself—

this was Jefferson, musing on the Ohio
from his Virginia,

where he sat in the guise of himself,
a pink reticular foam

enamored in *pelf*
or pilfer from upland hardwood; or

I was relaxing and don't know why I was so intent to see the red shirt

I looked closer ... I saw the ear and the shoulder—

roll up from the dull green middle
muddier with spring

as if the witness's eyes rise out of the day

like the scribbling song
of a Bell's vireo

Sunday hunting the embayment
for concealed tags and elements

in the low-tempo tactical noon.

I followed the red to where it caught on a buoy

as the water was lavish
with melting rain.

Lack of proper sleep, overload,
and complacency

are three common errors of inattention.

Assume all guns are loaded
and be thoughtful of the wound channel
of full metal jacket

through bodies, walls, and the innocent.

I am a mom and I was born
in my drawerful of holsters

to free in others like me the genius loci
in that quick eddy.

What is situational awareness? To inspire and cultivate the discipline of looking—

sometimes simple as noting the location of a dumpster

while you pay for your groceries.

Note the slope angle of the coffee counter and
move along it

in rapid, handgun-based defense

for in the parking lot scenario
you are alone

and fate-bound to feel and dress
the run, hide, fight signals

at the nerve gates,

scribe by finger holographic shields in your personal space

for perception is a weapon of survival and behind every
    weapon is the survivor mind-set

within *the spread of threat*
at a picnic, with friends, driving

or whenever and wherever we gather
to make glorious this ancient afternoon,

protect our babies, our bodies,

and pleasure craft
on the Ohio's blue flow.

Let's take the boat

tired after work
and bounce these imaginary nations:

location, speed, direction of movement, posture, weapon
    state,

powerless to disprove the dark
that closes on the black willow and cottonwood

hiding the coal ash retention ponds.

From the water, pilot lights of single worlds
plot the line of dusk

scattered by rule to maintain distance
between all craft in this river's slow fall

to the touch of the Mississippi

where side by side these green and brown rivers
spiral for miles,

the Ohio's end

a perception too close
for any eye of recent memory

taken away

taken a

way.

Open Carry

That good will's shit to me

cheap deterrent
here in condition yellow
on Starbucks Appreciation Day.

Open carry says: *I'm this guy, and
this is my assault rifle,*

normal as a Coke and candy bar.

I may use my gun today,
a duty no more taxing

than traffic. Virtue is having the courage

to show what we're all thinking
with casual display.

As such conversations go, it may end
in the Roman courtesy to thank the Governor

for the order
of my execution,

I know, right, for the shooting will always be confused

and too late we shall see that

the real enemy is the Concealed Nation.
They are the ones hiding something.

Concealed Nations

A wind rotates
maple seeds on the sidewalk,
    weather

turns the radius of a song
        as two white men
stride roadside to Chipotle.

       This is the song
for what is concealed
        therein: a brittle, weightless wing.

Will you hold it
       to your lips
         and blow?

Hecuba

FOR AMIRI BARAKA

What is slave phenomenology?
Take your eyes from me

and step into
the common emptiness
sought for love.

Sores are open
Sunday.

It was this compass
that called freedom to appear

as she did, a ship drawing near, sunk by fire
and dragged in shore break,

and we a scrambled populace
vomiting the charry water and seaweed

that I, with my dog's head,
bow down to eat.

The Measure

On his bed of juicy grass, under the blue light
that burns around his fruit tree,

when I stand, a black-eyed dog stands
and sits

when I sit, and if I step forward
his teeth chatter and snap for the measure

he will not give.

Fall 2

Let the room collapse on our conversation, my friend. In you I see Saint Symeon, and our spot in the coffee queue will chance through the open window. Our body begins when the shoe trips on the folds of the floor. This poem is a scene of a middle-aged white male repeatedly failing to open a ketchup packet. *In statu degradationis,* I am compelled to climb the house to compass the meaning of my fall, to measure the blind violence vested in the gesture, the shared enemies that divided the street, its parcels, and the column of my fall.

The dramaturge seeks foolishness to become wise, reader, face down in the bushes, a space pressed into the gospel of captivity. I, too, came to read the virtuous aesthetics of our agony in the body passed out on the frozen grass strip between driveways as dawn breaks. There is only one subject of poetry: Join with the presence of a problem in society that may only be solved by a poem. So said Mayakovsky. That body, as artificial as hats, movies, or prayer, equally performs life. And, as we ask the poem to live, and we ask it to suffer creatively, to

wake shame
across this page, people and dogs
shit the pebbles
laid between strips of concrete

Ozzy and Wiz Khalifa collide
on blast
turn up

signal radii of palm tree pollen
stung with stars
and spider

the windless avenues
of California come to light

nude gum trees

welcome broken hearts

with not much going on
in the data

    the data the data is spraying the shrine
in hostile new encounters

calcium aerosol aloft
aspirating shell and polyethylene

the dead air our rental opens to

the vanishing search for the miraculous

Science Is Suffering

Frog model controls for unexpected death may be prevented from leaving the study with a little foil

lid.

Comment on the Emission Spectrum

The principle challenge in mouse intestine
is not the darkness inside the body
but the excitability of the native light
residing in all tissue.

We send flares and everything shines,
drowning desired signals
in febrile color dreams
of false positive.

The problem is beyond biology.
Perhaps the spectrum desires miscibility,
a self-corrective return
to an unknown monophylum.

You will find, to come out with it,
that experimental lighting of cell death
ends in a kind of cream
attempting to digest your finger.

Reproducibility Zoo

Alzheimer's Disease: Mouse

Amyotrophic Lateral Sclerosis: Frog

Huntington's Disease: Pig

Depression: Rabbit

Fatty Liver: Mouse

Migraine: Hamster

Multiple Sclerosis: Hamster

Pain: Mouse

Parkinson's Disease: House Fly

Spinal Cord Injury: Rabbit

Stroke & Brain Ischemia: Mouse

Traumatic Brain Injury: Mouse

Anxiety: Rat or Mouse

This Poem Takes Privileges

I can ably say
the people light upwards

so we are luminous

                                      bow's

as the rain-   bloom

Infant with Love

I felt you watching
and kicked the air,

wheeled the sand,
my hands dried by salt.

A man is a leap—
contrapposto on the beach—

and where there is one
therein many.

See them out there to their knees.

Lights in the ocean.

    The cartilaginous
and bony fish.

Kill Chain

FOR ABDULRAHMAN AL-AWLAKI

Glass-eyed drones compete for light
solo hours too frictionless to store

maintained driveways
and ordinary occupations
that can bear the pain.

Have you learned yet
how to filter the sunset? Read it as a mirror's steam

and where there's smoke there's volume

for objects in derivative places,
sounds, holes, shadows,

the mere siren
a signal.

Trust the aids for human agents,
and when doubtful recall that all observation

is indirect
from your seat. Think of the work
as setting the fasting table,

grinding the alike parts
with under-sensed artificial hands.

The screen will learn,
and if the deceivers be true
the light of the sun will break

and a formless ocean will fall
from the sky.

When you clock out

they will all still be on that highway
and it will always be night

to limit the capture wedge

the screen senses as a bend in the bicycle bell

rang to bend the road
of this passing world.

In an unseen room hinged to this one

autonomous grains of rice
seek to understand
what I am looking at

and why I stroke and pet the reserve
in the animal I keep.

We are together, this reserve and I,
a system that long abandoned intelligence

to model instead the brain
sensing the changing light

on the rotated apple.

Insert card and remove quickly.

The big hill home is a coincidence
of figs and grapes in the darkness,

preemptive strategies of physical or mechanical,

anxieties of labor
in un-bordered time.

Should you sway to madness, imagine scallops
passed this way on the timeline,

one tenth of one second
within a day of evolution,

this 1 /
19 / 71,

a life
cycle from selector to target.

We are born without the right to be forgotten,

I read the next morning,

before I am pulled away
by a spider thread

strung from the bus seat back
to my hand.

I was here as the landscape
writing itself on the way to work

and wondered

why should the volume of this moment
not explode?

Two forms of intelligence are required
to grant the strike authority

whisker and fingertip.

Do you ask yourself
how fast you can evacuate

stolen opportunities for prayer?

The data are an entity
primed for terror in a thousand scenarios

in the drag this morning of the rain band's long tail
over the propensity field.

It's not what happened but what might have
or could
pass between the house and

the bodies asleep
in the state of humiliation.

What is the person
the prison system wants you to be?

I rise and lie beside the children
as my body becomes the house,

the haunt of the dream
where we used to live.

Autumn already! Let us pine for the sunshine
as heaven is built from light,

mused the pilot, as we take this opportunity

to acknowledge the men and women of signals intelligence:

the work they do is working
or we wouldn't be flying this morning,

so his prayer
was repeated silently in the rows,

a thin shadow of the plane passing
a threat falling on houses and roads

for my part lost in imagining a letter to a friend I wish
I could tell how parts of me are changing.

It strikes me:
parts of my body, my right leg,
my left foot,

can still really fly,

if witness accounts are to be believed,
parts of bodies
erupting in force

into the tinsel and vanilla cream clouds
with no edging,

the day cast
kind of pink.

Corn, cattle, and automobile-related,
the demand of evidence

is replicability—

so kids stripped off windbreakers
and ran to the corner store,
April 4,
coughing with the cold.

My hands dip into the frame
to re-button the coat,
sweep the curl back from the face—

it is a living thing,
is it not, the poem,

if held at arm's length,

I do not know how to love it
with the love that I know now.

No, you may not touch me,

you may not see
my eyes

and if you find a blank page
it does not indicate lack of need

to obscure the higher-touch mentor models
accounting the holy and the good.

Steppes of ochre rock
cool in a mined landscape

elsewhere on Earth;

here, pickled ginger and compact junk

tremble the infinite within
the bone of my arm,

as the proteins of the parking lot
fluoresce, green.

I feel my belly rising and falling,
the task regressed into smaller bites.

Live chromosomes
are ripped down the spindle

to record how a wound will revenge itself
within the system

to awaken the female body
and deal with it

in the neighboring office park,

freshwater canals
connecting the sea by hand.

I am seen here automating
realms of common activity

in an outline that lays the future city
on this one the crows

will not forget.

Why should it not explode

on a dizzy windshield,
the white sun data pump

of cedar tips seen first
from the fog's numinous breath, as
frost withdraws to leaf

and the beacons of wireless
sweep?

Hizzy leads to ten networks named
Home, then KingPooky's

UltraPookyNetwork
where perhaps the King is roused
from his ultra network
by the brittle tree rooted in his ear,

a rustle you hear only in heating vents
too low to be beneath the root,

thievery of all sorts
lost between targeting windows.

I wake and I play
the phone video of my son
before kill/capture operations
obliterated the garden

and its walls and
the words that covered other words
on the walls.

The word *Dabiq* writ
on each wall of the strip mall

now demolished. Do you remember it?

The word was *unicorns,*
cool cars, video games,
it was *rats and foreign ogres,*

Rumiyah and all
buried

in home, kids, and dinner,

words that need you
to memorize the chain

for engaging and enabling
the oculus of a soda straw

to behold migrations of hand-sewn and -crafted
animals protected from models
of the irrational.

Stand up from your chair,
stretch, and repeat:

You are here to make life as short as possible
for our enemies

in whatever propensity
you become.

All souls are in fall
or rising

inside the data,

and if we see each other at all,
it is only as we pass.

So I saw my body merge layers
without seed or root

the union of loss and gain
close what I become,

a body made
from what I have not done

and do, inside the light
of the glass eye.

On the climb of the big hill home
my son asks what a sunset is,
and I say it's that sun, the one beyond my finger,
but better;

you won't be allowed to see it,

as you will be asleep, and if you don't sleep,
you won't be happy.

None should desensitize to the alert crawl,

as you are made from its numberless
jewel eyes

and may not speak interference
with the ability to kill or capture

a single, multicellular, soft-bodied animal
waiting to explode
at the heart's gate.

When the data shake hands
shoot to kill.

Broward

You have to understand it is tribal, driven by race. That's Florida. I was the white kid that said, Hey, I fixed the lawnmower, maybe I can be a mechanic. Cars are bigger there than anywhere, and every race had their type. We were into '80s Japanese cars. I did some college anyway not realizing what a waste it is. I did political science. There wasn't really an industry to sign up for in Broward outside of politics. It's the most important piece for Florida, and the parties and the campaigns, down to the glorified copyboys, employ people with the dollars pouring in from outside. I went to Al Gore's speech in Miami the night before the 2000 election. Worst time of my life. We were fenced in and I waited eight hours pressed against these people trying not to piss down my pant leg. After all that, Gore came out and spoke for ten minutes like people were excited about equality. A couple days later he lost the election because of Florida. I left feeling sick with how smug they were; they thought they had that election. A Democrat will never win Florida again in my lifetime. They don't get that progressive politics mean nothing to immigrants. Cubans, Haitians,

Black Miami, Dominicans. All the South Americans have their own thing. There is no politics but everybody getting after the money for ourselves or our people. So I did the Navy, and now that I work here, I can say the only things I care about are ultimate fighting and stand-up. I do spend a lot time lifting. It's just a job. I don't care about looking good. It's from something I read once about a girl that was raped. I read how she was saying she was helpless to stop it. So I lift. Nothing scares me like being overpowered. I remember being a skinny guy. I go on and off all kind of supplements. People don't understand how hard it is to chase any gains. The body gets used to anything. I'd take steroids if my kidneys weren't shot. I would rather die than be raped. But that's not my biggest fear. You know what I fear? With my luck I'll die in a fire. That might be the last thing I'm afraid of. Because I don't know how I fight that. Fire ends it.

Finished, he yawned. I said, *So the only fear left is being raped by fire?* He smiled and said, *and Hillary.* I stood up, a common tactic to end workplace conversation or hide a broken heart. This was winter of 2016. He left the office to pursue an MBA and soon stopped returning my e-mails.

Walking Stick

*We didn't protest. It's not like
you're going to get anything from
anybody. They don't have it either.
And the new system moves
pretty quick—*

I found a feral walking stick
stripped from a tree
by a June shower
nursing trumpets
of crumpled lilac

and held her scarlet eye
on the outpatient
pharmacy line—

If the breadth of the difficulty
rejects one ardent name,

I may still call the hour
a phasmid or phantom,
freely stealing my heart
from the other needs
that burn it.

Innertown

Theft and sleep
phased to a mono
alarm.
This is the disposition
of sympathy
rousing the city.
I'm awake and
I'm fine.
How they were
I can't read.

Burn it Up (after Sappho)

And how he got into that straw raincoat
                                      I don't know.

Our bare feet crushed rings in the clover
and you turned to present the moment to me
as if our bower were an altar—sweet boy;

I say nothing
to watch you speak

as the house finch lights
the dawn.

Stephen Crane

I came upon a man.
I said my glasses make pictures
of my hands. I look at them
as if my eyes were decanters, as if
my hands are sensible.

I'm sure it's brutal to see on
occasion, he said, but I am blind

and nine of my fingers are cut
to the stub.

Whose Blues

Will your bare arms
spread out in mine,
as if the center of the Milky Way
had not collapsed
millions of years before
this senseless day turned
down the mergers and coalitions of
Alberta Street,
less and less
              in mind?

Fall 3

Friends had organized a benefit for *LVNG*, a free poetry magazine in Chicago, in 1994. I was to read with a couple others in Pilsen, a Mexican immigrant community, then unthreatened by white gentrification. *LVNG* was unknown in Pilsen, but this discontinuity appealed to the inchoate motives of the white poets of our group. We'll read there because we're unknown, we thought. The new Café Jumping Bean, opened by Latino artists, was itself unique among the *lavanderias,* dollar stores, pay-day loan shops, and torta venders of 18th Street. A bitter wind scoured the filthy snow from bright blue to gray to black. A raised platform for performances backed to floor length windows on 18th Street. Personal friends accounted for nearly all of the audience when the reading began. I read some imitative verse styled after the dramaturgical lyrics of *Personae*, the typewritten sheets trembling, if you looked closely, in my hand.

As I read, a man caked in hand-gathered coat rags appeared out of the freezing night to press himself right up against

EL MARIACHI

Brass ring of
the flared lip, the note's
sharp edge tears along
the high steps, trills down.
My love in my eyes
steps away, twirls
a loop, her
eyes snap back to mine.
The horns wave to the night.
Blowing out his cheeks,
El mariachi sweats
in his collar,
his eyes squeezed shut.

the window behind me, contesting the poems in phlegmy bursts of glass-dampened Spanish. From my one glance backwards, I remember most vividly the towering hat made from the cheap nylon caps you could get on the street for a dollar, piled one after another into a thick ball atop his head. My voice had no hope of competing with his, but I didn't pause, even as I heard the long streaks of his hands drawn down the glass and his laughter. I pressed forward, catching the eyes in the audience and raising my voice, as if the crisis of the moment was the threat of not being able to hear the poems, and the natural response was to protect the poem. I was also oddly excited by the anxiety in the room. To stop reading seemed like admitting that poetry was too precious for the mad violence our environment makes; I was responsible for the desire of the audience not to be humiliated along with me. But what, I ask you now, was being humiliated in that moment? Competing forms of violence came to a contest that poetry mastered by refusing. I believe I sensed then that it could only be I who was humiliated. It wasn't humiliating simply that I could not foresee the exercise of mastery in my limited imagination, nor that I felt safe to conjure a nameless mariachi through a lyric poem performed in the Mexican neighborhood. The humiliation was to see how distant the crucible of my lyric imagination was from the real. But there, in the real time of that realization, I was aware of some thrill of undressing the autonomy of my imagination. The presumption that poetry resides in the anterior of the social contest was removed and the poem was pushed onto an uncanny bridge between what urged the poem to be and what came to meet it: the two forces forming the unconcealed violence art is born within. Exposed on that bridge, I had the first feeling that poetry was rightly born in humiliation. Afterward, I asked a friend what the guy had been doing behind me. *Jeering, or maybe "japing" is the word, I don't know what to call it,* he said. *Whatever he was saying, he was really into it. I tried not to keep looking away. Then he just left.*

Western Avenue

In the great green room,
things are softly moistened

each time you leave.

Feels like never
this rain will get here

the weatherman said;
to me, in my still bed,

again.

[. . .] AQUI VIVE

A meaty dog named Donkey lives
outside my apartment door.

I hear his toenails on the tile when
he clambers to his feet and lies down again.

May he never abandon me.

I Dreamed I Saw
Ron Johnson Last Night

We spoke of the impermanent
and the permanent
walking the corn aisle
in steady time if

never introduced
between two tones,
white and blue.

We searched for a better lighter
without a childproof spring.   *Press*

this latch down to the wheel that grinds the flint
and imagine your thumb is thin as a ghost's.

Nude nerves alight inside the body's panoply

and *the words that startled the water*
from the un-graven state

its utmost manifold

that sends one no place

where holy flowers ring

                        the cedar drum.

You Are Surrounded!

Do not try to imagine the furniture; there is none,

no comity in abandoned hours
as the competition never stops, as I imagine

my adversary, irrationalized far away
and graced by bouncing clouds,

as I record beneath the desk
this nude day.

Landscape with Fill
(after Joseph Ceravolo)

The hills and margarine
spread the environs out
as if our hairiness cannot not accumulate
fine, hydrogenated
                flecks of fat.

Where may I find the proper body

beneath this harvest moon in yellow ailanthus,
pulled by cable
thru the hole in the wall and
inescapable?

"eat shit beef"

FOR TOM, AGAIN

Shrimp & Pork eyeball
home penetration

caritas and clarity
left in the car

onward to the exit of time
birds turn into birds
different seeming in intelligence and habit

natural gases that could do more with suzerainty

as the giant finger folds back the pink gills
in the sky

happy to leave the study of
how the Earth used today

to get over

itself

Downriver

I grew up by the train tracks, on a dead-end street a few miles from the gas refineries. Some of the round tanks we'd drive past were cheerfully painted with stitching to look like giant baseballs. The refineries stood between us and the car factories on Detroit's southwest side. The trains that passed the house were almost white noise; they never sped, just rolled by with newly manufactured sedans and wagons. The steel rails would bend down, stretched by the weight of the train cars, making a low, dull grinding sound punctuated by tight squeaks of the wheels. We played up there freely—it was the park. The fist-sized rocks of the rail bed were terrific missiles. The Fords and Cadillacs in the car caissons were unprotected, factory-new. We tried to crack as many windows and windshields in a railcar before it got by. I don't know why we did it; we had formed no opinions of property or pride, nor urge to protest the product our area survived on. Breaking the glass was just what the imagination provided. The form that makes the mind. I've not added much to this. The page is the glass I'm trying to break.

Poem for Tearing Away

Crab blossom stripped
by trawls of rain—

March flow
of putrescible materials
follow me down

to watch this poem
drink from the drain.

Notes

"Tutor Song"

The poem does not lie /... / this hour
John Wieners, "A poem for tea heads," *The Hotel Wentley Poems*, The Auerhahn Press, 1958.

"Voice Box"

Arrest me, if I run away
This line takes liberties with *tene me quia fugi*, reportedly tattooed on the forehead of slaves in the Roman Empire. See Petronius's novel, *Satyricon*, and Christopher J. Fuhrmann, *Policing the Roman Empire: Soldiers, Administration, and Public Order*, Oxford University Press, 2012.

"I WAS. I AM NOT. I DON'T CARE."

I WAS. I AM NOT. I DON'T CARE.
Harold Mattingly, *Christianity in the Roman Empire*, W.W. Norton, 1967.

one man's hair comb /... /... cents
The Blues Brothers, dir. John Landis, 1980.

"How Many Bubbles Are in a Bar of Soap?"

How many bubbles are in a bar of soap?
Example of a "literacy" test that required "correct" answers to be granted the right to vote. These nonsensical questions targeted black community polling places in Alabama and Mississippi prior to the Voting Rights Act of 1965.

"Love Songs of Military Anthropology"

It's a long wait / ... / success in war
For further reading on fresh produce availability and the potential spread of terror groups in post-war Iraq, see Marcus Griffin, "An Anthropologist among the Soldiers," in John D. Kelly, Beatrice Jauregui, Sean T. Mitchell, and Jeremy Walton, editors, *Anthropology and Global Counterinsurgency*, University of Chicago Press, 2010.

"Concealed Carry"

anastomoses, scallops, rills, flutes, spongework, boxwork, pendants, and human remains
Kentucky cave protections law KRS 433.871(7-8).

whether the black of the negro resides in the reticular membrane between the skin and scarf-skin, or in the scarf-skin itself—
Thomas Jefferson, *Notes on the State of Virginia*, 1785.

I was relaxing ... shoulder
I followed the red ... buoy

Molly Born, "Investigators Now Ask: What Led to Death of Missing Duquesne Student?" *Pittsburgh Post-Gazette*, online. Accessed January 2017. This poem also quotes from a video interview with the woman who first spotted the body in the river posted online to accompany the article.

> *sometimes simple ... dumpster.*
>
> *the spread of threat / ... / we gather*

"What is Situational Awareness" published at ConcealedNation.com. Accessed January 2017.

"Open Carry"

> *I'm this guy. ... normal as a Coke and candy bar*

"I am all for the 2nd but don't like concealed carry, and this is why ..." discussion board post by Punisher75 at AboveTop Secret.com. Accessed January 2017.

"Science Is Suffering"

> *Frog model / ... / may be prevented with a little foil*

Adapted from "Making & Injecting Embryos Based on Gerhart Lab Protocols," Klymkowsky Lab, University of Colorado, Boulder (online). Accessed January 2017.

"Kill Chain"

> *.... make life as short as possible*

These lines and more echo from "The Drone Papers," published at The Intercept (online). Accessed January 2017. *Dabiq* and *Ru-*

miyah were publications of the Islamic State of Iraq and the Levant (ISIL) published online between 2014 and 2017.

"Broward"

Conversation with work colleague, 2016.

"Fall 2"

In statu degradationis
Saint Ignatius on the body: "the state of humiliation."

the data the data is spraying the shrine
Edward Dorn, *Gunslinger*. 50th anniversary ed., Duke University Press, 2018.

"[…] AQUI VIVE"

[…] AQUI VIVE
Fading billboard, Chicago, product illegible. Likely "Tecate," which did and does live there.

"eat shit beef"

eat shit beef
Tom Raworth, "History Portrayed by Lifesize Working Models," in *Windmills in Flames*. Carcanet, 2010.

Acknowledgments

"Walking Stick" first appeared in *The Nation*. "Love Songs of Military Anthropology" was contained in a poem entitled "Married at the Mouth" that first appeared in *Chicago Review*. "Infant with Love" first appeared in *LVNG* Magazine #8: "The Great Lakes Issue." Several others were published online by *Gramma*. Many thanks to the editors of these publications.

Images

Figure 1: Bas Jan Ader, seated in a small wooden chair on the roof of the house he rents in Los Angeles in 1970. Photo taken during the filming of "Fall 1, Los Angeles," a short film by Bas Jan Ader (1970). © The Estate of Bas Jan Ader / Mary Sue Ader Andersen, 2019 / The Artists Rights Society (ARS), New York. Courtesy of Meliksetian | Briggs, Los Angeles.

Figure 2: Bas Jan Ader falling from the chair, the chair tumbling along behind his body, about halfway down the roof of the rented house in Los Angeles. Photo taken during the filming of "Fall 1, Los Angeles," a short film by Bas Jan Ader (1970). © The Estate of Bas Jan Ader / Mary Sue Ader Andersen, 2019 / The Artists Rights Society (ARS), New York. Courtesy of Meliksetian | Briggs, Los Angeles.

Figure 3: Bas Jan Ader, free, tumbles off the roofline of the porch, his right leg wildly splayed in the effort to protect himself from the fall. The chair may be caught on the roofline of the sheltered entryway of the house that he rents. Photo taken during the filming of "Fall 1, Los Angeles," a short film by Bas Jan Ader (1970). © The Estate of Bas Jan Ader / Mary Sue Ader Andersen, 2019 / The Artists Rights Society (ARS), New York. Courtesy of Meliksetian | Briggs, Los Angeles.

Figure 4: Bas Jan Ader, nearing the ground, has twisted to face the camera, seeking to land feet first as his body lands in the bushes in front of the Los Angeles house that he rents. The chair remains stuck in the crook of the roofline between perch and entryway. Photo taken during the filming of "Fall 1, Los Angeles," a short film by Bas Jan Ader (1970). © The Estate of Bas Jan Ader / Mary Sue Ader Andersen, 2019 / The Artists Rights Society (ARS), New York. Courtesy of Meliksetian | Briggs, Los Angeles."

Figure 5: Scan of typewritten poem (1994), "El Mariachi," by Joel Felix. Courtesy of Michael O'Leary.

Joel Felix lives near the Salish Sea with Junot, Sanchaman, and Candice Rai.